D0607030

50 Quick & Easy Pizzas

Step-by-Step

50 Quick & Easy Pizzas

Shirley Gill

Photography by Karl Adamson

Acropolis
Books

First published in 1995 by Lorenz Books

© Anness Publishing Limited 1995

Lorenz Books is an imprint of
Anness Publishing Limited
1 Boundary Row
London SE1 8HP

Distributed in Australia by Reed Editions

All rights reserved. No part of this publication may be
reproduced, stored in a retrieval system, or transmitted in
any way or by any means, electronic, mechanical,
photocopying, recording or otherwise, without the prior
permission of the copyright holder.

ISBN 1 85967 091 1

A CIP catalogue record is available from the British Library.

Publisher: Joanna Lorenz
Series Editor: Joanne Rippin
Designer: Peter Laws
Jacket Designer: Peter Butler
Photographer: Karl Adamson

MEASUREMENTS
Three sets of equivalent measurements have been provided in the recipes here, in
the following order: Metric, Imperial and American. It is essential that units of
measurement are not mixed within each recipe. Where conversions result in
awkward numbers, these have been rounded for convenience, but are accurate
enough to produce successful results.

Typeset by MC Typeset Ltd, Rochester, Kent
Printed and bound in Hong Kong

CONTENTS

INTRODUCTION

The pizza originated as a cheap, savoury snack in Naples, sold from street stalls or in special eating houses, but it has long since been upgraded to a universally popular main meal. Today's favourite fast food, pizzas are quick and filling meals for people in a hurry. However, if you take the time to make your own you will find they are easy and fun – the simplest are often the best, provided the ingredients are fresh and flavoursome. They are suitable for all tastes, with toppings that have become far more generous and varied than the traditional Italian pizzas.

In this book you will find instructions on how to make basic pizza dough as well as several delicious alternatives. The amount of dough needed for one recipe is small and very easy to handle, and preparations are simple and straightforward. If using ready-made bases, these recipes can be made in less than one hour.

A word on baking pizzas: the very best results are achieved by cooking them in a traditional brick oven to make them light and crisp. Even without a brick oven, the home cook can achieve excellent results with a pizza brick and it is well worth buying one if you make pizzas frequently. The direct heat makes them wonderfully crisp. Pizzas must be eaten hot straight from the oven as they soon harden in an unappetizing way.

Pizzas need not be served just as snacks or main meals; they can become stylish starters, when they are made as small pizzettes or served in thin wedges. They also make great party food – a festive array of pizzas will please any crowd!

This is a collection for pizza lovers everywhere. Although most of the recipes contain cheese, this can be reduced if you desire a lighter pizza. There is also a final section of interesting Italian breads, full of great flavours and textures just waiting to be tasted.

Herbs and Spices

Herbs and spices are essential for seasoning pizzas and improving their flavour. Fresh herbs should be used whenever possible. Buy growing herbs in pots: this not only ensures the herbs are as fresh as possible, but also provides a continuous supply.

Basil (sweet basil)
Intensely aromatic, basil has a distinctive peppery flavour. The leaves can be used to garnish pizzas and are also ideal with tomato in a summer salad; chopped or shredded it can become the main seasoning ingredient.

Black peppercorns
Black peppercorns are best used freshly ground in a mill or crushed as the taste and aroma disappears quickly.

Chillies (fresh and dried chilli products)
Fresh chillies vary in taste, from mild to fiery hot. Generally the large, round fleshy varieties are milder than the small, thin-skinned pointed ones. For a milder, spicy flavour, remove the seeds and veins.

Red chilli flakes are made from dried, crushed chillies and are somewhat milder than fresh chillies. They can be heated with olive oil to make chilli oil for brushing over pizza bases or used to add bite to pizza toppings and fillings for calzone.

Mild chilli powder is a commercially prepared mixture of chilli, ground herbs and spices. It can be used to flavour more contemporary-styled pizzas.

Chives
A member of the onion family, the long, narrow green leaves are best used as a garnish or snipped and added to the pizza dough for extra flavour.

Coriander
The delicate light green leaves have an unusual flavour and distinctive aroma. Chopped leaves are often used in combination with chillies, especially in Californian-style pizzas. The fresh leaves also make an attractive garnish.

Cumin
These seeds have a warm, earthy flavour and aromatic fragrance and are sold whole or ground. Use in pizzas, especially those with chilli and oregano, for a Mexican flavour.

Curly parsley
This provides colour and gives a fresh flavour to pizza toppings.

Flat-leaf parsley
This variety has much more flavour than common curly parsley, but they can be used interchangeably.

Herbes de Provence
A dried herb mixture of thyme, savory, rosemary, marjoram and oregano. It is especially good mixed with black olives and added to pizza doughs or sprinkled on top before cooking.

Nutmeg
Nutmeg has a sweetish, highly aromatic flavour which has an affinity for rich foods. It is used to great effect in stuffed pizzas and pizza toppings, especially those containing spinach.

Oregano
An aromatic and highly flavoured herb. Oregano features strongly in Italian cooking, where it is sprinkled on to pizzas.

Rosemary
Rosemary, with its dark green, needle-like leaves, can be overpowering, but when used judiciously, it can add a delicious flavour to vegetables like potatoes for an unusual pizza topping.

Saffron
The dried stigmas of the saffron crocus, saffron is the most expensive spice in the world, but fortunately very little is needed in most recipes, sometimes as little as a pinch. Pungent with a brilliant yellow colour, saffron is available as strands or ground.

Sage
Just a few leaves can deliciously flavour a pizza topping, especially with a rich-tasting cheese like Gorgonzola; sage tends to overpower subtle flavours.

Salt
Salt balances the action of yeast and is an integral part of bread-making. For seasoning, use sea salt flakes or refined table salt; the former has a slightly stronger flavour so use it sparingly.

Thyme
This is excellent chopped or crumbled, and stirred into tomato sauce or sprinkled on to pizzas. Whole sprigs can be used as a garnish.

saffron

red chilli flakes

coriander

mild chilli powder

fresh red chillies

chives

thyme

curly parsley

flat-leaf parsley

ground cumin

herbes de Provence

nutmeg

sage

rosemary

oregano

basil

black peppercorns

sea salt

Fresh Vegetables for Pizzas

Never has vegetable cookery been so exciting. A quick glance in the greengrocers and super-markets reveals a remarkable choice. There are baby aubergines, wild mushrooms, red onions, colourful peppers, hot-tasting chillies, as well as fennel and wonderful asparagus – a truly international offering, providing endless possibilities to the cook.

As vegetables are so full of colour they make attractive and tempting pizza toppings. Choose the best quality fresh vegetables for maximum flavour and scout around to see what is newly in season. Get to know which of them should be pre-cooked – mushrooms, courgettes and aubergines for example – and which can be used raw – onions, leek and tomato slices. Vegetable pizzas are not just for vegetarians; they are for everyone who enjoys exciting food, inventively prepared and presented with style.

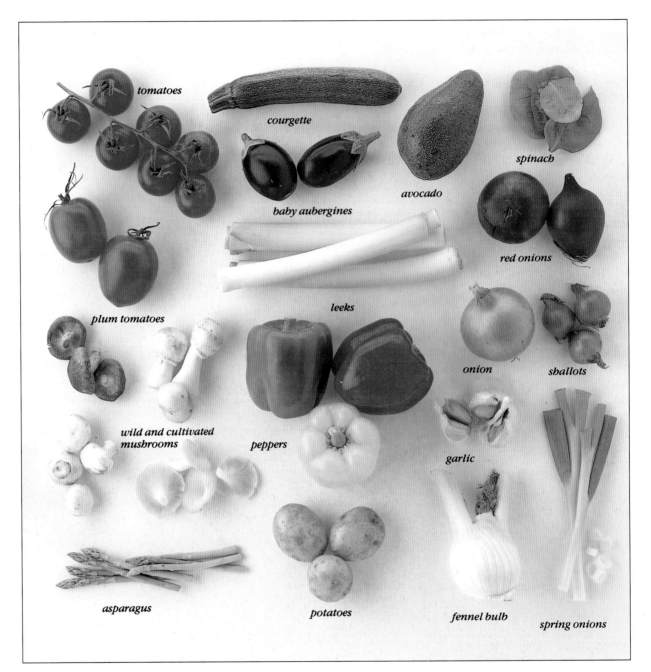

tomatoes

courgette

spinach

avocado

baby aubergines

red onions

plum tomatoes

leeks

onion   shallots

wild and cultivated
mushrooms

peppers

garlic

asparagus

potatoes

fennel bulb

spring onions

Meat and Fish for Pizzas

Pizzas with a meat or fish topping make a marvellous substantial lunch or supper dish served with tossed salad leaves. They can be topped with a wealth of delicious ingredients. Sliced cured meats, salamis, ham and sausages are popular favourites. Look for them in supermarkets where they may be either pre-packed in the chilled cabinets or at the delicatessen counter. Chicken and minced beef can also be used in highly imaginative ways.

Fresh fish and shellfish also make tempting pizza toppings. Favourites such as prawns, mussels, squid and salmon may be used alone or mixed for a good variety of flavours. Canned fish such as tuna and anchovies are also an important feature of pizza toppings. If you find anchovies too salty, it helps to soak them in milk before use. For best results, some shellfish are added halfway through the cooking time to ensure that they are not overcooked. When you are shopping for fish and shellfish the most important quality to look for is freshness.

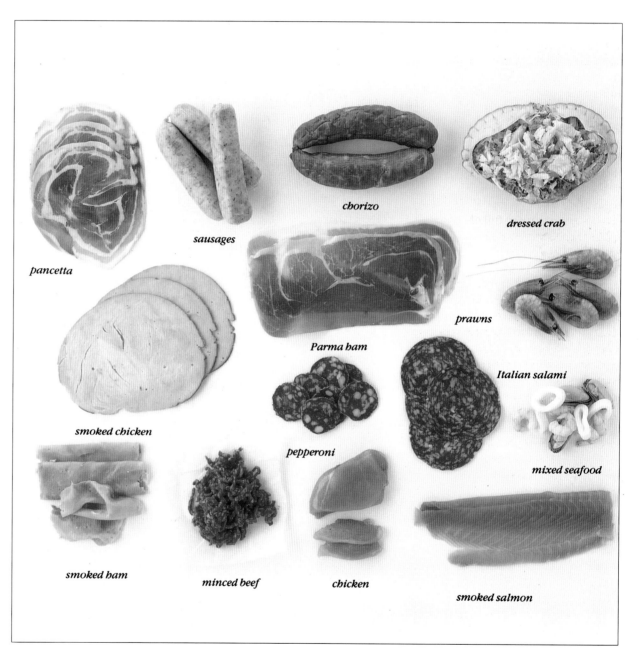

pancetta

sausages

chorizo

dressed crab

Parma ham

prawns

smoked chicken

Italian salami

pepperoni

mixed seafood

smoked ham

minced beef

chicken

smoked salmon

Storecupboard

For the most part the recipes in this book call upon fresh everyday ingredients and certain essential items from the storecupboard. There are a few specialist ingredients, however, which are worth hunting for. They may seem expensive, but just a little will go a long way to give your pizzas character and flair.

Anchovies
Canned anchovies imported from the Mediterranean have been filleted and salted before being packed in oil. They are an important flavouring ingredient and garnish for many pizzas.

Artichoke hearts
When these are specified in a recipe, those packed in oil in jars have been used. They are ideal for pizza toppings.

Capers
These are the flower buds of a shrub native to the Mediterranean which are preserved in vinegar and salt or salt alone. They have a strong piquant flavour and should be used with care.

Cornmeal (polenta flour)
Adds texture and an earthy flavour to the basic pizza dough.

Easy-blend dried yeast
Much faster and quicker to use than fresh or dried yeast, as its name implies. It does not need to be reconstituted in liquid first; but is mixed directly with the flour. Use lukewarm liquid to mix the dough as extreme temperatures can kill the yeast and the dough will not rise.

Flour
White flour contains 72–74 per cent of the wheat grain. It is available in strong, plain and self-raising forms.

Traditional pizza bases are made from bread dough, which is usually made with strong white flour. It is called strong because of its high gluten content. Some strong white flours are also bleached, so look for "unbleached" on the label for untreated flour.

Plain white flour is used to make focaccia, a flattish bread with various toppings.

Self-raising white flour has had leavening or raising agents added to it, and is suitable for a scone pizza base.

Wholemeal flour is simply flour milled from the whole grain with nothing added or taken away. Strong and self-raising wholemeal flours are used for making pizza doughs. You will find mixing it with white flour produces a dough lighter in colour and texture.

Olives
Green olives are unripe; black are fully ripe and have more flavour. They are widely available in many forms – whole or stoned, or stuffed with ingredients like pimientoes or anchovy fillets. You can buy them preserved in brine or oil, and they are used only in their preserved state. Stoned olives can be baked into bread or used as a garnish.

Olive oil
A "pure" olive oil of good quality is indispensable for making traditional Italian pizzas. Olive oil brushed on the dough and a drizzle over the topping offers flavour and also protection in the fierce heat of the oven. Ingredients such as garlic and chillies can be added to the oil to provide extra flavour. Extra virgin olive oil is usually a darker green and has a more intense flavour.

Pimiento
Pimiento is the Spanish word for pepper. The red variety is available packed whole into cans. Sweet flavoured, with a bright red colour, they are a useful storecupboard standby.

Pine nuts
These small, oval, creamy coloured nuts with a sweet flavour are much appreciated in the Mediterranean and Middle East. They may be sprinkled on to pizzas to add texture, or used in sauces such as pesto, which can be spread over the dough base for extra flavour.

Red pesto
A richly aromatic sauce combining pesto with sun-dried tomatoes. Delicious spread on to pizza bases or stirred into tomato sauce.

Sun-dried tomato paste
This has a richer, more intense flavour than ordinary tomato purée and makes a quick pizza topping. It also enriches sauces and gives a lovely colour.

Tapenade
This is made from green or black olives ground to a paste with a little olive oil and seasoning. Delicious spread on to pizza bases or spooned on top just before serving, it is especially good with pizzas containing goat's cheese.

Tomatoes: canned
No storecupboard should be without them! Canned tomatoes come either whole or chopped, ready for use in sauces and toppings.

Tomatoes: sun-dried in oil
Sun-dried tomatoes have a concentrated, salty flavour, which is excellent used in small quantities in breads and as a pizza topping. They can also be bought loose in their dry state but they will need to be soaked in warm water before use.

Tomato purée
Useful for adding colour, intensity and flavour to home-made tomato sauce.

Tuna
Canned tuna fish is usually packed in oil, brine or water. Its firm texture makes it a useful pizza topping.

Walnuts
Walnuts are excellent added to bread to serve with antipasti.

anchovies

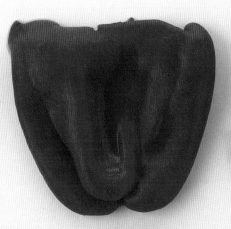

pimiento

walnuts

olive oil

sun-dried tomatoes

tuna

pine nuts

sun-dried tomato paste

artichoke hearts

capers

cornmeal

canned tomatoes

red pesto

black olives

green olives

easy-blend dried yeast

tomato purée

plain flour

black olive tapenade

green olive tapenade

wholemeal flour

strong white flour

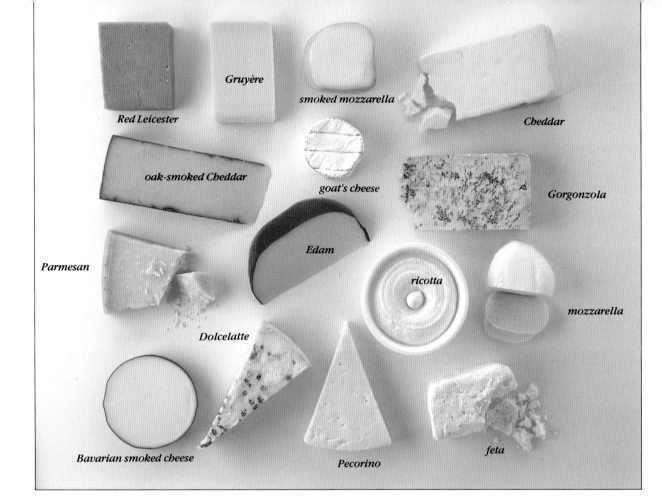

Gruyère
smoked mozzarella
Cheddar
Red Leicester
oak-smoked Cheddar
goat's cheese
Gorgonzola
Parmesan
Edam
ricotta
mozzarella
Dolcelatte
Bavarian smoked cheese
Pecorino
feta

Pizza Cheeses

One of the most important elements in the making of a tasty pizza is the cheese. Mozzarella is the cheese most often associated with pizza, but a variety of cheeses can be used, so experiment with different ones to suit your taste.

Bavarian smoked cheese
Sold in rounds with a brown wax coating, this cheese has a pale creamy colour and mild, smoky flavour with a smooth, soft texture.

Cheddar
This cow's milk cheese is considered England's most famous. Flavours can vary from mild to quite strong. It is a very versatile cheese, which is ideal for cooking with, since it doesn't draw threads and is universally popular.

Dolcelatte
An Italian blue-veined, semi-soft cheese. It has a smooth, creamy texture and delicate piquant flavour.

Edam
A Dutch ball-shaped cheese, firm and smooth in texture with a mild, nutty flavour.

Feta
Feta is a fairly hard cheese that crumbles easily on to pizzas. It is preserved in brine which accounts for its salty flavour. Rinse before using.

Goat's cheese
Goat's cheeses are small, generally shaped in logs, rounds, pyramids or ovals, and range in flavour from fresh and creamy to strong and tangy. They cook well and are especially good with roasted vegetables for a tasty vegetarian pizza.

Gorgonzola *piccante*
This cheese is pleasantly sharp in flavour, with a softish paste and blue-green veins.

Gruyère
A hard cheese with a distinctive sweet and nutty taste, it is widely used in cooking as a good melting cheese.

Mozzarella
This versatile cheese is used in many pizza recipes for its astounding melting quality. Good mozzarella should be very white, fairly elastic and moist when cut.

Oak-smoked Cheddar
A Cheddar variant which is excellent grated over pizzas, adding a distinctive flavour.

Parmesan
Italy's most famous hard cheese, which is usually grated for cooking and serving with pizza. Always buy fresh Parmesan if you can, as it is by far the best.

Pecorino
An Italian sheep's cheese which has a fairly strong distinctive flavour. It is used in the same way as Parmesan.

Red Leicester
This cheese has a mild flavour and bright colour.

Ricotta
A soft Italian whey cheese with a delicate, smooth flavour. It is ideal for use in fillings for calzone and panzerotti.

Smoked mozzarella
Smoked mozzarella has a creamy, smoky taste that gives it a more distinctive flavour than the plain variety. It also has excellent melting properties.

Equipment

To make pizzas successfully you do not have to have specialist tools, but tasks are made simpler with the aid of certain utensils and gadgets.

Baking sheet
Choose a large heavy baking sheet that will not warp at high temperatures.

Box grater
A multi-surfaced grater can be used for all grating purposes.

Cook's knife
This has a heavy, wide blade ideal for chopping.

Flour dredger
A useful piece of equipment for dusting the work surface.

Garlic press
This is a small metal gadget used for crushing garlic.

Measuring jug
Essential for measuring liquid, these jugs are available in a wide range of sizes.

Measuring spoons
Used for accurately measuring small amounts of ingredients.

Metal spoons
The best metal spoons are oval with a pointed end.

Mixing bowls
A set of bowls in various sizes is essential when cooking.

Nutmeg grater
This is a miniature grater used for grating whole nutmegs.

Rolling pin
Choose a long, heavy pin for even rolling.

Salt and pepper mills
These are used specifically for grinding coarse sea salt and whole peppercorns.

Swiss-roll tin
A rectangular tin, ideal for making hearty farmhouse pizzas.

Oil can
Usually made of metal it has a long, small spout for drizzling oil on to pizzas.

Olive stoner
This removes stones from olives with one quick press.

Paring knife
A small knife for trimming and peeling vegetables.

Parmesan grater
A special grater for Parmesan.

Pastry brush
This is useful for brushing on oil, water or beaten egg white.

Pastry cutter
This is used for stamping out dough rounds.

Pizza brick (Pizza stone)
A terracotta round, used instead of a baking sheet or pizza pan. The brick absorbs and retains heat, and crisps the dough.

Pizza cutter/lifter
A dual-purpose gadget for cutting and serving pizzas.

Pizza pan
Traditional pizza pans are round and shallow. Deep-pan pizza tins are also available, but a sandwich tin may be used instead. A perforated pizza pan allows steam to escape and encourages a crisp base.

Pizza wheel
This large cutting wheel is useful for easy slicing.

Wooden spoons
Essential in all kitchens is a set of wooden spoons.

Basic Pizza Dough

This simple bread base is rolled out thinly for a traditional pizza recipe.

MAKES
1 × 25–30 cm/10–12 in round pizza base
4 × 13 cm/5 in round pizza bases
1 × 30 × 18 cm/12 × 7 in oblong pizza base

INGREDIENTS
175 g/6 oz/1½ cups strong white flour
1.25 ml/¼ tsp salt
5 ml/1 tsp easy-blend dried yeast
120–150 ml/4–5 fl oz/½–⅔ cups lukewarm water
15 ml/1 tbsp olive oil

1 Sift the flour and salt into a large mixing bowl.

2 Stir in the yeast.

3 Make a well in the centre of the dry ingredients. Pour in the water and oil and mix with a spoon to a soft dough.

4 Knead the dough on a lightly floured surface for about 10 minutes until smooth and elastic.

5 Place the dough in a greased bowl and cover with clear film. Leave in a warm place to rise for about 1 hour or until the dough has doubled in size.

6 Knock back the dough. Turn on to a lightly floured surface and knead again for 2–3 minutes. Roll out as required and place on a greased baking sheet. Push up the dough to make a rim. The dough is now ready for topping.

Deep-pan Pizza Dough

This recipe produces a deep and spongy base.

MAKES
1 × 25 cm/10 in deep-pan pizza base

INGREDIENTS
225 g/8 oz/2 cups strong white flour
2.5 ml/½ tsp salt
5 ml/1 tsp easy-blend dried yeast
150 ml/¼ pint/⅔ cup lukewarm
   water
30 ml/2 tbsp olive oil

Follow the method for Basic Pizza Dough. When the dough has doubled in size, knock back and knead for 2–3 minutes. Roll out the dough to fit a greased 25 cm/10 in deep-pan pizza tin or sandwich tin. Let the dough prove for 10 minutes, then add the topping. Alternatively, shape and place on a greased baking sheet.

Wholemeal Pizza Dough

INGREDIENTS
75 g/3 oz/¾ cup strong wholemeal
   flour
75 g/3 oz/¾ cup strong white flour
1.25 ml/¼ tsp salt
5 ml/1 tsp easy-blend dried yeast
120–150 ml/4–5 fl oz/½–⅔ cup
   lukewarm water
15 ml/1 tbsp olive oil

Follow the method for Basic Pizza Dough. You may have to add a little extra water to form a soft dough, depending on the absorbency of the flour.

Cornmeal Pizza Dough

INGREDIENTS
175 g/6 oz/1½ cups strong white
   flour
25 g/1 oz/¼ cup cornmeal
1.25 ml/¼ tsp salt
5 ml/1 tsp easy-blend dried yeast
120–150 ml/4–5 fl oz/½–⅔ cup
   lukewarm water
15 ml/1 tbsp olive oil

Follow the method for Basic Pizza Dough.

Scone Pizza Dough

The joy of using a scone mixture is it's quick to make and uses storecupboard ingredients.

MAKES
1 × 25 cm/10 in round pizza base
1 × 30 × 18 cm/12 × 7 in oblong
   pizza base

INGREDIENTS
115 g/4 oz/1 cup self-raising flour
115 g/4 oz/1 cup self-raising
   wholemeal flour
pinch of salt
50 g/2 oz/4 tbsp butter, diced
about 150 ml/¼ pint/⅔ cup milk

1 Mix together the flours and salt in a mixing bowl. Rub in the butter until the mixture resembles fine breadcrumbs.

2 Add the milk and mix with a wooden spoon to a soft dough.

3 Knead lightly on a lightly floured surface until smooth. The dough is now ready to use.

Superquick Pizza Dough

If you're really pressed for time, try a packet pizza dough mix. For best results roll out the dough to a 25–30 cm/10–12 in circle; this is slightly larger than stated on the packet, but it does produce a perfect thin, crispy base. For a deep-pan version use two packets.

ALSO MAKES
4 × 13 cm/5 in round pizza bases
1 × 30 × 18 cm/12 × 7 in oblong
   pizza base

INGREDIENTS
1 × 150 g/5 oz packet pizza base mix
120 ml/4 fl oz/½ cup lukewarm water

1 Empty the contents of the packet into a mixing bowl.

2 Pour in the water and mix with a wooden spoon to a soft dough.

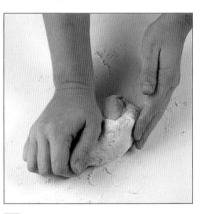

3 Turn the dough on to a lightly floured surface and knead for 5 minutes until smooth and elastic. The dough is now ready to use.

Using a Food Processor

For speed make the pizza dough in a food processor; let the machine do the mixing and kneading, then leave the dough to prove until doubled in size.

1 Put the flour, salt and yeast into a food processor. Process to mix.

2 Measure the water into a jug and add the oil. With the machine running, add the liquid and process until the dough forms a soft ball. Leave to rest for 2 minutes, then process for 1 minute more to knead the dough.

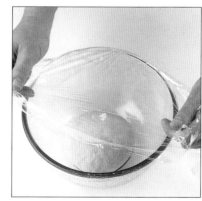

3 Remove the dough from the processor and shape into a neat round. Place in a greased bowl and cover with clear film. Leave in a warm place for about 1 hour until doubled in size. Knock back and knead the dough for 2–3 minutes. The dough is now ready to use.

Ready-made Pizza Bases

Fortunately for the busy cook it is now possible to buy fresh, frozen or long-life pizza bases from most supermarkets. Many are enriched with additional ingredients like cheese, herbs and onions. Although they never seem to taste as good as a real home-made pizza base they can be very useful to keep on hand. All you have to do is add your chosen topping and bake in the usual way.

Stoning Olives

Using a stoner is the easiest way to remove the stone from an olive, but you can also use a sharp knife.

1 Put the olive in the stoner, pointed end uppermost.

2 Squeeze the handles together to extract the stone.

Chopping Herbs

Use this method to chop herbs until they are as coarse or fine as you wish.

1 Strip the leaves from the stalk and pile them on a chopping board.

2 Using a sharp knife cut the herbs into small pieces, holding the tip of the blade against the board and rocking the blade back and forth.

Tomato Sauce

Tomato sauce forms the basis of the topping in many of the recipes. Make sure it is well seasoned and thick before spreading it over the base. It will keep fresh in a covered container in the fridge for up to 3 days.

COVERS
1 × 25–30 cm/10–12 in round pizza base
1 × 30 × 18 cm/12 × 7 in oblong pizza base

INGREDIENTS
15 ml/1 tbsp olive oil
1 onion, finely chopped
1 garlic clove, crushed
1 × 400 g/14 oz can chopped tomatoes
15 ml/1 tbsp tomato purée
15 ml/1 tbsp chopped fresh mixed herbs, such as parsley, thyme, basil and oregano
pinch of sugar
salt and black pepper

1 Heat the oil in a pan, add the onion and garlic and gently fry for about 5 minutes until softened.

2 Add the tomatoes, tomato purée, herbs, sugar and seasoning.

3 Simmer, uncovered, stirring occasionally for 15–20 minutes or until the tomatoes have reduced to a thick pulp. Leave to cool.

Flavoured Oils

For extra flavour brush these over the pizza base before adding the topping. They also form a kind of protective seal that keeps the crust crisp and dry.

CHILLI
INGREDIENTS
150 ml/¼ pint/⅔ cup olive oil
10 ml/2 tsp tomato purée
15 ml/1 tbsp dried red chilli flakes

1 Heat the oil in a pan until very hot but not smoking. Stir in the tomato purée and red chilli flakes. Leave to cool.

2 Pour the chilli oil into a small jar or bottle. Cover and store in the fridge for up to 2 months (the longer you keep it the hotter it gets).

GARLIC
INGREDIENTS
3–4 whole garlic cloves
120 ml/4 fl oz/½ cup olive oil

1 Peel the garlic cloves and put them into a small jar or bottle.

2 Pour in the oil, cover and refrigerate for up to 1 month.

Margherita

(Tomato, Basil and Mozzarella)
This classic pizza is simple to prepare. The sweet flavour of sun-ripe tomatoes works wonderfully with the basil and mozzarella.

Serves 2–3

INGREDIENTS
1 pizza base, about 25–30 cm/10–12 in
    diameter
30 ml/2 tbsp olive oil
1 quantity Tomato Sauce
150 g/5 oz mozzarella
2 ripe tomatoes, thinly sliced
6–8 fresh basil leaves
30 ml/2 tbsp freshly grated Parmesan
black pepper

basil

mozzarella

Parmesan

olive oil

Tomato Sauce

tomatoes

1 Preheat the oven to 220°C/425°F/ Gas 7. Brush the pizza base with 15 ml/ 1 tbsp of the oil and then spread over the Tomato Sauce.

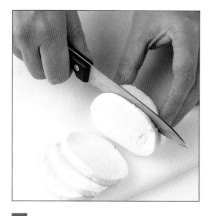

2 Cut the mozzarella into thin slices.

3 Arrange the sliced mozzarella and tomatoes on top of the pizza base.

4 Roughly tear the basil leaves, add and sprinkle with the Parmesan. Drizzle over the remaining oil and season with black pepper. Bake for 15–20 minutes until crisp and golden. Serve immediately.

Marinara

(Tomato and Garlic)
The combination of garlic, good quality olive oil and oregano give this pizza an unmistakably Italian flavour.

Serves 2–3

INGREDIENTS
60 ml/4 tbsp olive oil
675 g/1½ lb plum tomatoes, peeled, seeded and chopped
1 pizza base, about 25–30 cm/10–12 in diameter
4 garlic cloves, cut into slivers
15 ml/1 tbsp chopped fresh oregano
salt and black pepper

olive oil

oregano

plum tomatoes

garlic

1 Preheat the oven to 220°C/425°F/Gas 7. Heat 30 ml/2 tbsp of the oil in a pan. Add the tomatoes and cook, stirring frequently for about 5 minutes until soft.

2 Place the tomatoes in a sieve and leave to drain for about 5 minutes.

3 Transfer the tomatoes to a food processor or blender and purée until smooth.

4 Brush the pizza base with half the remaining oil. Spoon over the tomatoes and sprinkle with garlic and oregano. Drizzle over the remaining oil and season. Bake for 15–20 minutes until crisp and golden. Serve immediately.

Quattro Stagioni

(Four Seasons)
This traditional pizza is divided into quarters, each with a different topping to depict the four seasons of the year.

Serves 2–4

INGREDIENTS
45 ml/3 tbsp olive oil
50 g/2 oz button mushrooms, sliced
1 pizza base, about 25–30 cm/10–12 in
   diameter
1 quantity Tomato Sauce
50 g/2 oz Parma ham
6 pitted black olives, chopped
4 bottled artichoke hearts in oil,
   drained
3 canned anchovy fillets, drained
50 g/2 oz mozzarella, thinly sliced
8 fresh basil leaves, shredded
black pepper

artichoke hearts

mozzarella

olive oil

Tomato Sauce

Parma ham

basil

button mushrooms

black olives

anchovy fillets

1 Preheat the oven to 220°C/425°F/ Gas 7. Heat 15 ml/1 tbsp of the oil in a frying pan and fry the mushrooms until all the juices have evaporated. Leave to cool.

2 Brush the pizza base with half the remaining oil. Spread over the Tomato Sauce and mark into four equal sections with a knife.

3 Arrange the mushrooms over one section of the pizza.

4 Cut the Parma ham into strips and arrange with the olives on another section.

5 Thinly slice the artichoke hearts and arrange over a third section. Halve the anchovies lengthways and arrange with the mozzarella over the fourth section.

6 Scatter over the basil. Drizzle over the remaining oil and season with black pepper. Bake for 15–20 minutes until crisp and golden. Serve immediately.

Napoletana

(Tomato, Mozzarella and Anchovies)
This pizza is a speciality of Naples. It is both one of the simplest to prepare and the most tasty.

Serves 2–3

INGREDIENTS
1 pizza base, about 25–30 cm/10–12 in
  diameter
30 ml/2 tbsp olive oil
6 plum tomatoes
2 garlic cloves, chopped
115 g/4 oz mozzarella, grated
50 g/2 oz can anchovy fillets, drained
  and chopped
15 ml/1 tbsp chopped fresh oregano
30 ml/2 tbsp freshly grated Parmesan
black pepper

Parmesan

mozzarella

anchovy fillets

olive oil

plum tomatoes

garlic

oregano

1 Preheat the oven to 220°C/425°F/ Gas 7. Brush the pizza base with 15 ml/ 1 tbsp of the oil. Put the tomatoes in a bowl and pour over boiling water. Leave for 30 seconds, then plunge into cold water.

2 Peel, seed and roughly chop the tomatoes. Spoon the tomatoes over the pizza base and sprinkle over the garlic.

3 Mix the mozzarella with the anchovies and scatter over.

4 Sprinkle over the oregano and Parmesan. Drizzle over the remaining oil and season with black pepper. Bake for 15–20 minutes until crisp and golden. Serve immediately.

Quattro Formaggi

(Four Cheeses)

Rich and cheesey, these individual pizzas are quick to assemble, and the aroma of melting cheese is irresistible.

Serves 4

INGREDIENTS
1 quantity Basic or Superquick Pizza
   Dough
15 ml/1 tbsp Garlic Oil
½ small red onion, very thinly sliced
50 g/2 oz Dolcelatte
50 g/2 oz mozzarella
50 g/2 oz Gruyère, grated
30 ml/2 tbsp freshly grated Parmesan
15 ml/1 tbsp chopped fresh thyme
black pepper

red onion

mozzarella

Parmesan

Garlic Oil

Dolcelatte

Gruyère

thyme

1 Preheat the oven to 220°C/425°F/ Gas 7. Divide the dough into four pieces and roll out each one on a lightly floured surface into a 13 cm/5 in circle. Place well apart on two greased baking sheets, then push up the dough edges to make a thin rim. Brush with Garlic Oil and top with the red onion.

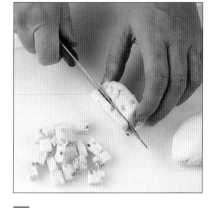

2 Cut the Dolcelatte and mozzarella into cubes and scatter over the bases.

3 Mix together the Gruyère, Parmesan and thyme and sprinkle over.

4 Grind over plenty of black pepper. Bake for 15–20 minutes until crisp and golden and the cheese is bubbling. Serve immediately.

Fiorentina

Spinach is the star ingredient of this pizza. A grating of nutmeg to heighten its flavour gives this pizza its unique character.

Serves 2–3

INGREDIENTS
175 g/6 oz fresh spinach
45 ml/3 tbsp olive oil
1 small red onion, thinly sliced
1 pizza base, about 25–30 cm/10–12 in diameter
1 quantity Tomato Sauce
freshly grated nutmeg
150 g/5 oz mozzarella
1 size 3 egg
25 g/1 oz Gruyère, grated

mozzarella

Gruyère

Tomato Sauce

spinach

red onion

nutmeg

egg

1 Preheat the oven to 220°C/425°F/Gas 7. Remove the stalks from the spinach and wash the leaves in plenty of cold water. Drain well and pat dry with kitchen paper.

2 Heat 15 ml/1 tbsp of the oil and fry the onion until soft. Add the spinach and continue to fry until just wilted. Drain off any excess liquid.

3 Brush the pizza base with half the remaining oil. Spread over the Tomato Sauce, then top with the spinach mixture. Grate over some nutmeg.

4 Thinly slice the mozzarella and arrange over the spinach. Drizzle over the remaining oil. Bake for 10 minutes, then remove from the oven.

5 Make a small well in the centre and drop the egg into the hole.

6 Sprinkle over the Gruyère and return to the oven for a further 5–10 minutes until crisp and golden. Serve immediately.

American Hot

This popular pizza is spiced with green chillies and pepperoni.

Serves 2–3

INGREDIENTS

1 pizza base, about 25–30 cm/10–12 in
   diameter
15 ml/1 tbsp olive oil
115 g/4 oz can peeled and chopped
   green chillies in brine, drained
1 quantity Tomato Sauce
75 g/3 oz sliced pepperoni
6 pitted black olives
15 ml/1 tbsp chopped fresh oregano
115 g/4 oz mozzarella, grated
oregano leaves, to garnish

mozzarella

oregano

Tomato Sauce

pepperoni

olive oil

green chillies

black olives

1 Preheat the oven to 220°C/425°F/ Gas 7. Brush the pizza base with the oil.

2 Stir the chillies into the sauce, and spread over the base.

3 Scatter over the pepperoni.

4 Halve the olives lengthways and scatter over, with the oregano.

5 Sprinkle over the grated mozzarella and bake for 15–20 minutes until the pizza is crisp and golden.

VARIATION

You can make this pizza as hot as you like. For a really fiery version use fresh red or green chillies, cut into thin slices, in place of the chillies in brine.

6 Garnish with oregano leaves and serve immediately.

Prosciutto, Mushroom and Artichoke

Here is a pizza full of rich and varied flavours. For a delicious variation use mixed cultivated mushrooms.

Serves 2–3

INGREDIENTS
1 bunch spring onions
60 ml/4 tbsp olive oil
225 g/8 oz mushrooms, sliced
2 garlic cloves, chopped
1 pizza base, about 25–30 cm/10–12 in
　　diameter
8 slices prosciutto *di speck*
4 bottled artichoke hearts in oil,
　　drained and sliced
60 ml/4 tbsp freshly grated Parmesan
salt and black pepper
thyme sprigs, to garnish

spring onions

Parmesan

mushrooms

prosciutto

olive oil

artichoke hearts

1 Preheat the oven to 220°C/425°F/ Gas 7. Trim the spring onions, then chop all the white and some of the green stems.

2 Heat 30 ml/2 tbsp of the oil in a frying pan. Add the spring onions, mushrooms and garlic and fry over a moderate heat until all the juices have evaporated. Season and leave to cool.

3 Brush the pizza base with half the remaining oil. Arrange the prosciutto, mushrooms and artichoke hearts on top.

4 Sprinkle over the Parmesan, then drizzle over the remaining oil and season. Bake for 15–20 minutes. Garnish with thyme sprigs and serve immediately.

Chorizo and Sweetcorn

The combination of spicy chorizo and sweet, tender corn works well in this hearty and colourful pizza. For a simple variation you could use chopped fresh basil instead of flat-leaf parsley.

Serves 2–3

INGREDIENTS

1 pizza base, about 25–30 cm/10–12 in
   diameter
15 ml/1 tbsp Garlic Oil
1 quantity Tomato Sauce
175 g/6 oz chorizo sausages
175 g/6 oz (drained weight) canned
   sweetcorn kernels
30 ml/2 tbsp chopped fresh flat-leaf
   parsley
50 g/2 oz mozzarella, grated
30 ml/2 tbsp freshly grated Parmesan

Tomato Sauce

mozzarella

flat-leaf parsley

Garlic Oil

chorizo sausages

Parmesan

 sweetcorn

1 Preheat the oven to 220°C/425°F/ Gas 7. Brush the pizza base with Garlic Oil and spread over the Tomato Sauce.

2 Skin and cut the chorizo sausages into chunks and scatter over the Tomato Sauce. Bake for 10 minutes then remove from the oven.

3 Sprinkle over the sweetcorn and flat-leaf parsley.

4 Mix together the mozzarella and Parmesan and sprinkle over. Bake for a further 5–10 minutes until crisp and golden. Serve immediately.

Chilli Beef

Minced beef, red kidney beans and smoky cheese combined with oregano, cumin and chillies give this pizza a Mexican character.

Serves 4

INGREDIENTS
30 ml/2 tbsp olive oil
1 red onion, finely chopped
1 garlic clove, crushed
½ red pepper, seeded and finely
    chopped
175 g/6 oz lean minced beef
2.5 ml/½ tsp ground cumin
2 fresh red chillies, seeded and
    chopped
115 g/4 oz (drained weight) canned
    red kidney beans
1 quantity Cornmeal Pizza Dough
1 quantity Tomato Sauce
15 ml/1 tbsp chopped fresh oregano
50 g/2 oz mozzarella, grated
75 g/3 oz oak-smoked Cheddar, grated
salt and black pepper

Tomato Sauce

red onion

minced beef

mozzarella

oak-smoked Cheddar

red chillies

oregano

olive oil

red kidney beans

red pepper

1 Preheat the oven to 220°C/425°F/ Gas 7. Heat 15 ml/1 tbsp of the oil in a frying pan, add the onion, garlic and pepper and gently fry until soft. Increase the heat, add the beef and brown well, stirring constantly.

2 Add the cumin and chillies and continue to cook, stirring, for about 5 minutes. Add the beans and seasoning.

3 Roll out the dough on a surface dusted with cornmeal and use to line a 30 × 18 cm/12 × 7 in greased Swiss-roll tin. Push up the dough edges to make a rim.

4 Spread over the Tomato Sauce.

5 Spoon over the beef mixture then scatter over the oregano.

6 Sprinkle over the cheeses and bake for 15–20 minutes until crisp and golden. Serve immediately.

VARIATION

If you prefer a milder version of this spicy pizza, reduce the amount of fresh chillies or leave them out altogether.

Chicken, Shiitake Mushroom and Coriander

The addition of shiitake mushrooms adds an earthy flavour to this colourful pizza, while fresh red chilli adds a hint of spiciness.

Serves 3–4

INGREDIENTS

45 ml/3 tbsp olive oil
350 g/12 oz chicken breast fillets, skinned and cut into thin strips
1 bunch spring onions, sliced
1 fresh red chilli, seeded and chopped
1 red pepper, seeded and cut into thin strips
75 g/3 oz fresh shiitake mushrooms, wiped and sliced
45–60 ml/3–4 tbsp chopped fresh coriander
1 pizza base, about 25–30 cm/10–12 in diameter
15 ml/1 tbsp Chilli Oil
150 g/5 oz mozzarella
salt and black pepper

chicken breast fillets

spring onions

red chilli

coriander

red pepper

olive oil

Chilli Oil

shiitake mushrooms

1 Preheat the oven to 220°C/425°F/ Gas 7. Heat 30 ml/2 tbsp of the olive oil in a wok or large frying pan. Add the chicken, spring onions, chilli, pepper and mushrooms and stir-fry over a high heat for 2–3 minutes until the chicken is firm but still slightly pink within. Season.

2 Pour off any excess oil, then set aside the chicken mixture to cool.

3 Stir the fresh coriander into the chicken mixture.

4 Brush the pizza base with the chilli oil.

5 Spoon over the chicken mixture and drizzle over the remaining olive oil.

6 Grate the mozzarella and sprinkle over. Bake for 15–20 minutes until crisp and golden. Serve immediately.

Pancetta, Leek and Smoked Mozzarella

Smoked mozzarella with its brownish smoky-flavoured skin, pancetta and leeks make this an extremely tasty and easy-to-prepare pizza, ideal for a light lunch.

Serves 4

INGREDIENTS
30 ml/2 tbsp freshly grated Parmesan
1 quantity Basic or Superquick Pizza
  Dough
30 ml/2 tbsp olive oil
2 medium leeks
8–12 slices pancetta
150 g/5 oz smoked mozzarella
black pepper

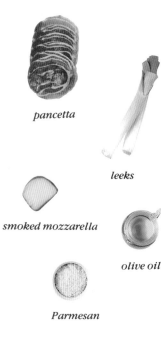

pancetta

leeks

smoked mozzarella

olive oil

Parmesan

1 Preheat the oven to 220°C/425°F/
Gas 7. Dust the work surface with the
Parmesan, then knead into the dough.
Divide the dough into four pieces and roll
out each one to a 13 cm/5 in circle. Place
well apart on two greased baking sheets,
then push up the edges to make a thin
rim. Brush with 15 ml/1 tbsp of the oil.

2 Trim and thinly slice the leeks.

3 Arrange the pancetta and leeks on
the pizza bases.

4 Grate the smoked mozzarella and
sprinkle over. Drizzle over the remaining
oil and season with black pepper. Bake
for 15–20 minutes until crisp and golden.
Serve immediately.

Ham and Mozzarella Calzone

A calzone is a kind of "inside-out" pizza – the dough is on the outside and the filling on the inside. For a vegetarian version replace the ham with sautéed mushrooms or chopped cooked spinach.

Serves 2

INGREDIENTS
1 quantity Basic or Superquick Pizza
  Dough
115 g/4 oz ricotta
30 ml/2 tbsp freshly grated Parmesan
1 egg yolk
30 ml/2 tbsp chopped fresh basil
75 g/3 oz cooked ham, finely chopped
75 g/3 oz mozzarella, cut into small
  cubes
olive oil for brushing
salt and black pepper

basil

ricotta

egg

mozzarella

Parmesan

cooked ham

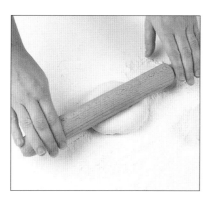

1 Preheat the oven to 220°C/425°F/ Gas 7. Divide the dough in half and roll out each piece on a lightly floured surface to an 18 cm/7 in circle.

2 In a bowl mix together the ricotta, Parmesan, egg yolk, basil and seasoning.

3 Spread the mixture over half of each circle, leaving a 2.5 cm/1 in border, then scatter the ham and mozzarella on top. Dampen the edges with water, then fold over the other half of dough to enclose the filling.

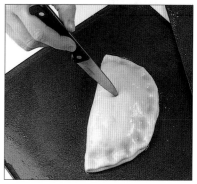

4 Press the edges firmly together to seal. Place on two greased baking sheets. Brush with oil and make a small hole in the top of each to allow the steam to escape. Bake for 15–20 minutes until golden. Serve immediately.

Smoked Chicken, Yellow Pepper and Sun-dried Tomato Pizzettes

These ingredients complement each other perfectly and make a really delicious topping.

Serves 4

INGREDIENTS
1 quantity Basic or Superquick Pizza
   Dough
45 ml/3 tbsp olive oil
60 ml/4 tbsp sun-dried tomato paste
2 yellow peppers, seeded and cut into
   thin strips
175 g/6 oz sliced smoked chicken or
   turkey, chopped
150 g/5 oz mozzarella, cubed
30 ml/2 tbsp chopped fresh basil
salt and black pepper

basil

mozzarella

yellow peppers

olive oil

smoked chicken

sun-dried tomato paste

1 Preheat the oven to 220°C/425°F/ Gas 7. Divide the dough into four pieces and roll out each one on a lightly floured surface to a 13 cm/5 in circle. Place well apart on two greased baking sheets, then push up the dough edges to make a thin rim. Brush with 15 ml/1 tbsp of the oil.

2 Brush the pizza bases generously with the sun-dried tomato paste.

3 Stir-fry the peppers in half the remaining oil for 3–4 minutes.

4 Arrange the chicken and peppers on top of the sun-dried tomato paste.

5 Scatter over the mozzarella and basil. Season with salt and black pepper.

VARIATION

For a vegetarian pizza with a similar smokey taste, omit the chicken, roast the yellow peppers and remove the skins before using, and replace the mozzarella with Bavarian smoked cheese.

6 Drizzle over the remaining oil and bake for 15–20 minutes until crisp and golden. Serve immediately.

Spicy Sausage

This is a tasty and substantial pizza. You may substitute fresh Italian spicy sausages, available from good Italian delicatessens, if you prefer.

Serves 3–4

INGREDIENTS

225 g/8 oz good quality pork sausages
5 ml/1 tsp mild chilli powder
2.5 ml/½ tsp freshly ground black pepper
30 ml/2 tbsp olive oil
2–3 garlic cloves
1 pizza base, about 25–30 cm/10–12 in diameter
1 quantity Tomato Sauce
1 red onion, thinly sliced
15 ml/1 tbsp chopped fresh oregano
15 ml/1 tbsp chopped fresh thyme
50 g/2 oz mozzarella, grated
50 g/2 oz freshly grated Parmesan

thyme and oregano

Tomato Sauce

red onion

Parmesan

mozzarella

olive oil

pork sausages

mild chilli powder

1 Preheat the oven to 220°C/425°F/ Gas 7. Skin the sausages by running a sharp knife down the side of the skins. Place the sausagemeat in a bowl and add the chilli powder and black pepper; mix well. Break the sausagemeat into walnut-sized balls.

4 Thinly slice the garlic cloves.

2 Heat 15 ml/1 tbsp of the oil in a frying pan and fry the sausage balls for 2–3 minutes until evenly browned.

5 Brush the pizza base with the remaining oil, then spread over the Tomato Sauce. Scatter over the sausages, garlic, onion and herbs.

3 Using a slotted spoon remove the sausage balls from the pan and drain on kitchen paper.

6 Sprinkle over the mozzarella and Parmesan and bake for 15–20 minutes until crisp and golden. Serve immediately.

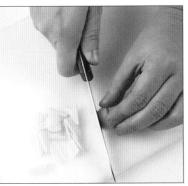

Caramelized Onion, Salami and Black Olive

The flavour of the sweet caramelized onion is offset by the salty black olives and herbes de Provence in the pizza base and the sprinkling of Parmesan to finish.

Serves 4

INGREDIENTS
700 g/1½ lb red onions
60 ml/4 tbsp olive oil
12 pitted black olives
1 quantity Basic or Superquick Pizza
    Dough
5 ml/1 tsp dried herbes de Provence
6–8 slices Italian salami, quartered
30–45 ml/2–3 tbsp freshly grated
    Parmesan
black pepper

Italian salami

olive oil

red onions

Parmesan

black olives

herbes de Provence

1 Preheat the oven to 220°C/425°F/ Gas 7. Thinly slice the onions.

2 Heat 30 ml/2 tbsp of the oil in a pan and add the onions. Cover and cook gently for 15–20 minutes, stirring occasionally until the onions are soft and very lightly coloured. Leave to cool.

3 Finely chop the black olives.

4 Knead the dough on a lightly floured surface, adding the black olives and herbes de Provence. Roll out the dough and use to line a 30 × 18 cm/12 × 7 in Swiss-roll tin. Push up the dough edges to make a thin rim and brush with half the remaining oil.

5 Spoon half the onions over the base, top with the salami and the remaining onions.

6 Grind over plenty of black pepper and drizzle over the remaining oil. Bake for 15–20 minutes until crisp and golden. Remove from the oven and sprinkle over the Parmesan to serve.

Ham and Pineapple French Bread Pizza

French bread makes a great pizza base. For a really speedy recipe use ready-prepared pizza topping instead of the Tomato Sauce.

Serves 4

INGREDIENTS
2 small baguettes
1 quantity Tomato Sauce
75 g/3 oz sliced cooked ham
4 rings canned pineapple, drained well and chopped
½ small green pepper, seeded and cut into thin strips
75 g/3 oz mature Cheddar
salt and black pepper

green pepper

mature Cheddar

pineapple

cooked ham

baguette

Tomato Sauce

1 Preheat the oven to 200°C/400°F/ Gas 6. Cut the baguettes in half lengthways and toast the cut sides until crisp and golden.

2 Spread the Tomato Sauce over the toasted baguettes.

3 Cut the ham into strips and arrange on the baguettes with the pineapple and pepper. Season.

4 Grate the Cheddar and sprinkle on top. Bake or grill for 15–20 minutes until crisp and golden.

Parma Ham, Roasted Peppers and Mozzarella Ciabatta Pizzas

Succulent roasted peppers, salty Parma ham and creamy mozzarella – the delicious flavours of these easy pizzas are hard to beat.

Serves 2

INGREDIENTS
½ loaf ciabatta bread
1 red pepper, roasted and peeled
1 yellow pepper, roasted and peeled
4 slices Parma ham, cut into thick
  strips
75 g/3 oz mozzarella
black pepper
tiny basil leaves, to garnish

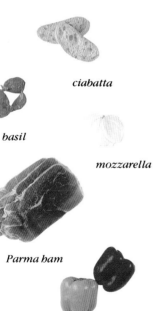

ciabatta

basil

mozzarella

Parma ham

red and yellow peppers

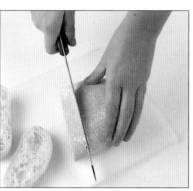

1 Cut the ciabatta bread into four thick slices and toast both sides until golden.

2 Cut the roasted peppers into thick strips and arrange on the toasted bread with the Parma ham.

3 Thinly slice the mozzarella and arrange on top. Grind over plenty of black pepper. Place under a hot grill for 2–3 minutes until the cheese is bubbling.

4 Arrange the basil leaves on top and serve immediately.

Pepperoni Pan Pizza

This pizza is made using a scone base which happily does not require proving! The topping can be varied to include whatever you like best – tuna fish, prawns, ham or salami are all good alternatives to the pepperoni.

Serves 2–3

INGREDIENTS

15 ml/1 tbsp chopped fresh mixed herbs
1 quantity Scone Pizza Dough
30 ml/2 tbsp tomato purée
400 g/14 oz can chopped tomatoes, drained well
50 g/2 oz button mushrooms, thinly sliced
75 g/3 oz sliced pepperoni
6 pitted black olives, chopped
50 g/2 oz Edam, grated
50 g/2 oz mature Cheddar, grated
15 ml/1 tbsp chopped fresh basil, to garnish

1 Add the herbs to the scone mix before mixing to a soft dough.

2 Turn the dough on to a lightly floured surface and knead lightly until smooth. Roll out to fit a well-greased frying pan, about 22 cm/8½ in diameter.

3 Cook the dough in the pan over a low heat for about 5 minutes until the base is golden. Lift carefully with a palette knife to check.

mature Cheddar

Edam

button mushrooms

chopped tomatoes

black olives

basil   *fresh mixed herbs*

pepperoni

 *tomato purée*

4 Turn the base on to a baking sheet, then slide it back into the pan, with the cooked side uppermost.

5 Mix together the tomato purée and drained tomatoes and spread over the pizza base. Scatter over the mushrooms, pepperoni, olives and cheeses. Continue to cook for about 5 minutes until the underside is golden.

6 When it is ready, transfer the pan to a preheated moderate grill for 4–5 minutes to melt the cheese. Scatter over the basil and serve immediately.

Mixed Seafood

Here is a pizza that gives you the full flavour of the
Mediterranean, ideal for a summer evening supper!

Serves 3–4

INGREDIENTS
1 pizza base, 25–30 cm/10–12 in
    diameter
30 ml/2 tbsp olive oil
1 quantity Tomato Sauce
400 g/14 oz bag frozen mixed cooked
    seafood (including mussels, prawns
    and squid), defrosted
3 garlic cloves
30 ml/2 tbsp chopped fresh parsley
30 ml/2 tbsp freshly grated Parmesan,
    to garnish

1 Preheat the oven to 220°C/425°F/
Gas 7. Brush the pizza base with 15 ml/
1 tbsp of the oil.

2 Spread over the Tomato Sauce. Bake
for 10 minutes. Remove from the oven.

3 Pat the seafood dry using kitchen
paper, then arrange on top.

mixed seafood

garlic

olive oil

parsley

Tomato Sauce

Parmesan

4 Chop the garlic and scatter over.

5 Sprinkle over the parsley, then drizzle over the remaining oil.

VARIATION

If you prefer, this pizza can be made with mussels or prawns on their own, or any combination of your favourite seafood.

6 Bake for a further 5–10 minutes until the seafood is warmed through and the base is crisp and golden. Sprinkle with Parmesan and serve immediately.

Salmon and Avocado

Smoked and fresh salmon make a delicious pizza topping when mixed with avocado. Smoked salmon trimmings are cheaper than smoked salmon slices and could be used instead.

Serves 3–4

INGREDIENTS
150 g/5 oz salmon fillet
120 ml/4 fl oz/½ cup dry white wine
1 pizza base, 25–30 cm/10–12 in diameter
15 ml/1 tbsp olive oil
400 g/14 oz can chopped tomatoes, drained well
115 g/4 oz mozzarella, grated
1 small avocado
10 ml/2 tsp lemon juice
30 ml/2 tbsp crème fraîche
75 g/3 oz smoked salmon, cut into strips
15 ml/1 tbsp capers
30 ml/2 tbsp snipped fresh chives, to garnish
black pepper

lemon

dry white wine

chopped tomatoes

mozzarella

avocado

smoked salmon

salmon fillet

crème fraîche

1 Preheat the oven to 220°C/425°F/ Gas 7. Place the salmon fillet in a frying pan, pour over the wine and season with black pepper. Bring slowly to the boil, remove from the heat, cover and cool. (The fish will cook in the cooling liquid.) Skin and flake the salmon into small pieces, removing any bones.

2 Brush the pizza base with the oil and spread over the drained tomatoes. Sprinkle over 50 g/2 oz of the mozzarella. Bake for 10 minutes, then remove from the oven.

3 Meanwhile, halve, stone and peel the avocado. Cut the flesh into small cubes and toss carefully in the lemon juice.

4 Dot teaspoonsful of the crème fraîche over the pizza base.

5 Arrange the fresh and smoked salmon, avocado, capers and remaining mozzarella on top. Season with black pepper. Bake for a further 5–10 minutes until crisp and golden.

6 Sprinkle over the chives and serve immediately.

Prawn, Sun-dried Tomato and Basil Pizzettes

Sun-dried tomatoes with their concentrated caramelized tomato flavour make an excellent topping for pizzas. Serve these pretty pizzettes as an appetizer or snack.

Serves 4

INGREDIENTS
1 quantity Basic or Superquick Pizza Dough
30 ml/2 tbsp Chilli Oil
75 g/3 oz mozzarella, grated
1 garlic clove, chopped
½ small red onion, thinly sliced
4–6 pieces sun-dried tomatoes, thinly sliced
115 g/4 oz cooked prawns, peeled
30 ml/2 tbsp chopped fresh basil
salt and black pepper
shredded basil leaves, to garnish

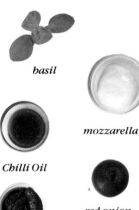

basil

mozzarella

Chilli Oil

red onion

sun-dried tomatoes

garlic

1 Preheat the oven to 220°C/425°F/ Gas 7. Divide the dough into eight pieces.

2 Roll out each one on a lightly floured surface to a small oval about 5 mm/¼ in thick. Place well apart on two greased baking sheets. Prick all over with a fork.

3 Brush the pizza bases with 15 ml/ 1 tbsp of the chilli oil and top with the mozzarella, leaving a 1 cm/½ in border.

4 Divide the garlic, onion, sun-dried tomatoes, prawns and basil between the pizza bases. Season and drizzle over the remaining chilli oil. Bake for 8–10 minutes until crisp and golden. Garnish with basil leaves and serve immediately.

Crab and Parmesan Calzonelli

These miniature calzone owe their popularity to their impressive presentation. If preferred, you can use prawns instead of crab.

Makes 10–12

INGREDIENTS
1 quantity Basic or Superquick Pizza Dough
115 g/4 oz mixed prepared crab meat, defrosted if frozen
15 ml/1 tbsp double cream
30 ml/2 tbsp freshly grated Parmesan
30 ml/2 tbsp chopped fresh parsley
1 garlic clove, crushed
salt and black pepper
parsley sprigs, to garnish

Parmesan

double cream

crab meat

parsley

garlic

1 Preheat the oven to 200°C/400°F/Gas 6. Roll out the dough on a lightly floured surface to 3 mm/⅛ in thick. Using a 7.5 cm/3 in plain round cutter stamp out 10–12 circles.

2 In a bowl mix together the crab meat, cream, Parmesan, parsley, garlic and seasoning.

3 Spoon a little of the filling on to one half of each circle. Dampen the edges with water and fold over to enclose filling.

4 Seal the edges by pressing with a fork. Place well apart on two greased baking sheets. Bake for 10–15 minutes until golden. Garnish with parsley sprigs.

Mussel and Leek Pizzettes

Serve these tasty seafood pizzettes with a crisp green salad for a light lunch.

Serves 4

INGREDIENTS
450 g/1 lb live mussels
120 ml/4 fl oz/½ cup dry white wine
1 quantity Basic or Superquick Pizza
  Dough
15 ml/1 tbsp olive oil
50 g/2 oz Gruyère
50 g/2 oz mozzarella
2 small leeks
salt and black pepper

olive oil

dry white wine

mozzarella

mussels

Gruyère

leeks

1 Preheat the oven to 220°C/425°F/ Gas 7. Place the mussels in a bowl of cold water to soak, and scrub well. Remove the beards and discard any mussels that are open.

2 Place the mussels in a pan. Pour over the wine, cover and cook over a high heat, shaking the pan occasionally, for 5–10 minutes until the mussels have opened.

3 Drain off the cooking liquid. Remove the mussels from their shells, discarding any that remain closed. Leave to cool.

4 Divide the dough into four pieces and roll out each one on a lightly floured surface to a 13 cm/5 in circle. Place well apart on two greased baking sheets, then push up the dough edges to form a thin rim. Brush the pizza bases with the oil. Grate the cheeses and sprinkle half evenly over the bases.

5 Thinly slice the leeks, then scatter over the cheese. Bake for 10 minutes, then remove from the oven.

VARIATION

Frozen or canned mussels can also be used, but will not have the same flavour and texture. Make sure you defrost the mussels properly.

6 Arrange the mussels on top. Season and sprinkle over the remaining cheese. Bake for a further 5–10 minutes until crisp and golden. Serve immediately.

Anchovy, Pepper and Tomato

This pretty, summery pizza is utterly simple, yet quite delicious. It's well worth grilling the peppers as they take on a lovely smoky flavour.

Serves 2–3

INGREDIENTS
6 plum tomatoes
45 ml/3 tbsp olive oil
5 ml/1 tsp salt
1 large red pepper
1 large yellow pepper
1 pizza base, 25–30 cm/10–12 in
   diameter
2 garlic cloves, chopped
50 g/2 oz can anchovy fillets, drained
black pepper
basil leaves, to garnish

olive oil

red and yellow peppers

plum tomatoes

garlic

anchovy fillets

1 Halve the tomatoes lengthways and scoop out the seeds.

2 Roughly chop the flesh and place in a bowl with 15 ml/1 tbsp of the oil and the salt. Mix well, then leave to marinate for 30 minutes.

3 Meanwhile, preheat the oven to 220°C/425°F/Gas 7. Slice the peppers in half lengthways and remove the seeds. Place the pepper halves, skin-side up, on a baking sheet and grill until the skins are evenly charred.

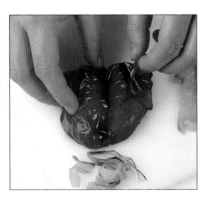

4 Place the peppers in a covered bowl for 10 minutes, then peel off the skins. Cut the flesh into thin strips.

5 Brush the pizza base with half the remaining oil. Drain the tomatoes, then scatter over the base with the peppers and garlic.

6 Snip over the anchovy fillets and season with black pepper. Drizzle over the remaining oil and bake for 15–20 minutes until crisp and golden. Garnish with basil leaves and serve immediately.

Tuna, Anchovy and Caper

This pizza makes a substantial supper dish which will provide two to three generous portions accompanied by a simple salad.

Serves 2–3

INGREDIENTS
1 quantity Scone Pizza Dough
30 ml/2 tbsp olive oil
1 quantity Tomato Sauce
1 small red onion
200 g/7 oz can tuna, drained
15 ml/1 tbsp capers
12 pitted black olives
45 ml/3 tbsp freshly grated Parmesan
50 g/2 oz can anchovy fillets, drained
   and halved lengthways
black pepper

Tomato Sauce

olive oil

Parmesan

black olives

tuna

red onion

capers

1 Preheat the oven to 220°C/425°F/ Gas 7. Roll out the dough on a lightly floured surface to a 25 cm/10 in circle. Place on a greased baking sheet and brush with 15 ml/1 tbsp of the oil. Spread the Tomato Sauce evenly over the dough.

2 Cut the onion into thin wedges and arrange on top.

3 Roughly flake the tuna with a fork and scatter over the onion.

4 Sprinkle over the capers, black olives and Parmesan.

5 Lattice the anchovy fillets over the top of the pizza.

6 Drizzle over the remaining oil, then grind over plenty of black pepper. Bake for 15–20 minutes until crisp and golden. Serve immediately.

Roasted Vegetable and Goat's Cheese

Here is a pizza which incorporates the smoky flavours of oven-roasted vegetables with the distinctive taste of goat's cheese.

Serves 3

INGREDIENTS
1 aubergine, cut into thick chunks
2 small courgettes, sliced lengthways
1 red pepper, quartered and seeded
1 yellow pepper, quartered and seeded
1 small red onion, cut into wedges
90 ml/6 tbsp Garlic Oil
1 pizza base, 25–30 cm/10–12 in diameter
1 × 400 g/14 oz can chopped tomatoes, drained well
1 × 115 g/4 oz goat's cheese (with rind)
15 ml/1 tbsp chopped fresh thyme
black pepper
green olive tapenade, to serve

courgettes

aubergine

goat's cheese

Garlic Oil

tapenade

chopped tomatoes

peppers

1 Preheat the oven to 220°C/425°F/ Gas 7. Place the aubergine, courgettes, peppers and onion in a large roasting tin. Brush with 60 ml/4 tbsp of the Garlic Oil. Roast for about 30 minutes until lightly charred, turning the peppers half-way through cooking. Remove from the oven and set aside.

2 When the peppers are cool enough to handle, peel off the skins and cut the flesh into thick strips.

3 Brush the pizza base with half the remaining Garlic Oil and spread over the drained tomatoes.

4 Arrange the roasted vegetables on top of the pizza.

5 Cube the goat's cheese and arrange on top. Scatter over the thyme.

COOK'S TIP

If you place the roasted peppers in a plastic bag while they cool, peeling off the skins becomes easier.

6 Drizzle over the remaining Garlic Oil and season with black pepper. Bake for 15–20 minutes until crisp and golden. Spoon the tapenade over to serve.

New Potato, Rosemary and Garlic

New potatoes, smoked mozzarella, rosemary and garlic make the flavour of this pizza unique. For a delicious variation, use sage instead of rosemary.

Serves 2–3

INGREDIENTS

350 g/12 oz new potatoes
45 ml/3 tbsp olive oil
2 garlic cloves, crushed
1 pizza base, 25–30 cm/10–12 in
   diameter
1 red onion, thinly sliced
150 g/5 oz smoked mozzarella, grated
10 ml/2 tsp chopped fresh rosemary
salt and black pepper
30 ml/2 tbsp freshly grated Parmesan,
   to garnish

olive oil

Parmesan

smoked mozzarella

new potatoes

rosemary

red onion

garlic

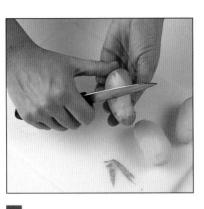

1 Preheat the oven to 200°C/425°F/ Gas 7. Cook the potatoes in boiling salted water for 5 minutes. Drain well. When cool, peel and slice thinly.

2 Heat 30 ml/2 tbsp of the oil in a frying pan. Add the sliced potatoes and garlic and fry for 5–8 minutes until tender.

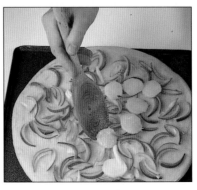

3 Brush the pizza base with the remaining oil. Scatter over the onion, then arrange the potatoes on top.

4 Sprinkle over the mozzarella and rosemary. Grind over plenty of black pepper and bake for 15–20 minutes until crisp and golden. Remove from the oven and sprinkle over the Parmesan to serve.

Wild Mushroom Pizzettes

Serve these extravagant pizzas as a starter. Fresh wild mushrooms add a distinctive flavour to the topping but a mixture of cultivated mushrooms such as shiitake, oyster and chestnut mushrooms would do just as well.

Serves 4

INGREDIENTS

45 ml/3 tbsp olive oil
350 g/12 oz fresh wild mushrooms,
    washed and sliced
2 shallots, chopped
2 garlic cloves, finely chopped
30 ml/2 tbsp chopped fresh mixed
    thyme and flat-leaf parsley
1 quantity Basic or Superquick Pizza
    Dough
40 g/1½ oz Gruyère, grated
30 ml/2 tbsp freshly grated Parmesan
salt and black pepper

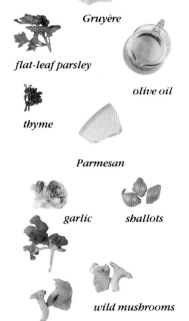

Gruyère

flat-leaf parsley

olive oil

thyme

Parmesan

garlic   *shallots*

wild mushrooms

1 Preheat the oven to 220°C/425°F/ Gas 7. Heat 30 ml/2 tbsp of the oil in a frying pan. Add the mushrooms, shallots and garlic and fry over a moderate heat until all the juices have evaporated.

2 Stir in half the herbs and seasoning, then set aside to cool.

3 Divide the dough into four pieces and roll out each one on a lightly floured surface to a 13 cm/5 in circle. Place well apart on two greased baking sheets, then push up the dough edges to form a thin rim. Brush the pizza bases with the remaining oil and top with the wild mushroom mixture.

4 Mix together the Gruyère and Parmesan, then sprinkle over. Bake for 15–20 minutes until crisp and golden. Remove from the oven and scatter over the remaining herbs to serve.

Chilli, Tomatoes and Spinach

This richly flavoured topping with a hint of spice makes a colourful and satisfying pizza.

Serves 3

INGREDIENTS
1–2 fresh red chillies
45 ml/3 tbsp tomato oil (from jar of
   sun-dried tomatoes)
1 onion, chopped
2 garlic cloves, chopped
50 g/2 oz (drained weight) sun-dried
   tomatoes in oil
400 g/14 oz can chopped tomatoes
15 ml/1 tbsp tomato purée
175 g/6 oz fresh spinach
1 pizza base, 25–30 cm/10–12 in
   diameter
75 g/3 oz smoked Bavarian cheese,
   grated
75 g/3 oz mature Cheddar, grated
salt and black pepper

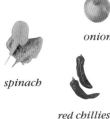

smoked Bavarian cheese

chopped tomatoes

mature Cheddar

sun-dried tomatoes

onion

garlic

spinach

red chillies

tomato oil

1 Seed and finely chop the chillies.

2 Heat 30 ml/2 tbsp of the tomato oil in a pan, add the onion, garlic and chillies and gently fry for about 5 minutes until they are soft.

3 Roughly chop the sun-dried tomatoes. Add to the pan with the chopped tomatoes, tomato purée and seasoning. Simmer uncovered, stirring occasionally, for 15 minutes.

4 Remove the stalks from the spinach and wash the leaves in plenty of cold water. Drain well and pat dry with kitchen paper. Roughly chop the spinach.

5 Stir the spinach into the sauce. Cook, stirring, for a further 5–10 minutes until the spinach has wilted and no excess moisture remains. Leave to cool.

6 Meanwhile, preheat the oven to 220°C/425°F/Gas 7. Brush the pizza base with the remaining tomato oil, then spoon over the sauce. Sprinkle over the cheeses and bake for 15–20 minutes until crisp and golden. Serve immediately.

Tomato, Pesto and Black Olive

These individual pizzas take very little time to put together. Marinating the tomatoes gives them extra flavour.

Serves 4

INGREDIENTS
2 plum tomatoes
1 garlic clove, crushed
60 ml/4 tbsp olive oil
1 quantity Basic or Superquick Pizza Dough
30 ml/2 tbsp red pesto
150 g/5 oz mozzarella, thinly sliced
4 pitted black olives, chopped
15 ml/1 tbsp chopped fresh oregano
salt and black pepper
oregano leaves, to garnish

red pesto

mozzarella

oregano

plum tomatoes

black olives

1 Slice the tomatoes thinly crossways, then cut each slice in half. Place the tomatoes in a shallow dish with the garlic. Drizzle over 30 ml/2 tbsp of the oil and season. Leave to marinate for 15 minutes.

2 Meanwhile, preheat the oven to 220°C/425°F/Gas 7. Divide the dough into four pieces and roll out each one on a lightly floured surface to a 13 cm/5 in circle. Place well apart on two greased baking sheets, then push up the dough edges to make a rim. Brush the pizza bases with half the remaining oil and spread over the pesto.

3 Drain the tomatoes, then arrange a fan of alternate slices of tomatoes and mozzarella on each base.

4 Sprinkle over the olives and oregano. Drizzle over the remaining oil on top and bake for 15–20 minutes until crisp and golden. Garnish with the oregano leaves and serve immediately.

Fresh Herb

Cut this pizza into thin wedges and serve as part of a mixed antipasti.

Serves 8

INGREDIENTS
115 g/4 oz mixed fresh herbs, such as
  parsley, basil and oregano
3 garlic cloves, crushed
120 ml/4 fl oz/½ cup double cream
1 pizza base, 25–30 cm/10–12 in
  diameter
15 ml/1 tbsp Garlic Oil
115 g/4 oz Pecorino, grated
salt and black pepper

double cream

Garlic Oil

Pecorino

basil

parsley

garlic

1 Preheat the oven to 220°C/425°F/
Gas 7. Chop the herbs, in a food
processor if you have one.

2 In a bowl mix together the herbs,
garlic, cream and seasoning.

3 Brush the pizza base with the Garlic
Oil, then spread over the herb mixture.

4 Sprinkle over the Pecorino. Bake for
15–20 minutes until crisp and golden and
the topping is still moist. Cut into thin
wedges and serve immediately.

Aubergine, Shallot and Sun-dried Tomato Calzone

Aubergines, shallots and sun-dried tomatoes make an unusual filling for calzone. Add more or less red chilli flakes, depending on personal taste.

Serves 2

INGREDIENTS
45 ml/3 tbsp olive oil
3 shallots, chopped
4 baby aubergines
1 garlic clove, chopped
50 g/2 oz (drained weight) sun-dried
  tomatoes in oil, chopped
1.25 ml/¼ tsp dried red chilli flakes
10 ml/2 tsp chopped fresh thyme
1 quantity Basic or Superquick Pizza
  Dough
75 g/3 oz mozzarella, cubed
salt and black pepper
15–30 ml/1–2 tbsp freshly grated
  Parmesan, to serve

Parmesan

thyme

mozzarella

olive oil

baby aubergines

shallots

red chilli flakes

1 Preheat the oven to 220°C/425°F/ Gas 7. Trim the aubergines, then cut into small cubes.

2 Cook the shallots until soft in a frying pan. Add the aubergines, garlic, sun-dried tomatoes, red chilli flakes, thyme and seasoning. Cook for 4–5 minutes, stirring frequently, until the aubergine is beginning to soften.

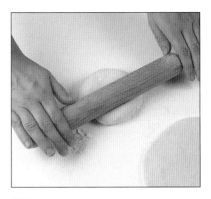

3 Divide the dough in half and roll out each piece on a lightly floured surface to an 18 cm/7 in circle.

4 Spread the aubergine mixture over half of each circle, leaving a 2.5 cm/1 in border, then scatter over the mozzarella.

5 Dampen the edges with water, then fold over the other half of dough to enclose the filling. Press the edges firmly together to seal. Place on two greased baking sheets.

6 Brush with half the remaining oil and make a small hole in the top of each to allow the steam to escape. Bake for 15–20 minutes until golden. Remove from the oven and brush with the remaining oil. Sprinkle over the Parmesan and serve immediately.

Tomato, Fennel and Parmesan

This pizza relies on the winning combination of tomatoes, fennel and Parmesan. The fennel adds both a crisp texture and a distinctive flavour.

Serves 2–3

INGREDIENTS
1 fennel bulb
45 ml/3 tbsp Garlic Oil
1 pizza base, 25–30 cm/10–12 in
  diameter
1 quantity Tomato Sauce
30 ml/2 tbsp chopped fresh flat-leaf
  parsley
50 g/2 oz mozzarella, grated
50 g/2 oz Parmesan, grated
salt and black pepper

mozzarella

flat-leaf parsley

Parmesan

Tomato Sauce

fennel bulb

Garlic Oil

1 Preheat the oven to 220°C/425°F/ Gas 7. Trim and quarter the fennel lengthways. Remove the core and slice thinly.

2 Heat 30 ml/2 tbsp of the Garlic Oil in a frying pan and sauté the fennel for 4–5 minutes until just tender. Season.

3 Brush the pizza base with the remaining Garlic Oil and spread over the Tomato Sauce. Spoon the fennel on top and scatter over the flat-leaf parsley.

4 Mix together the mozzarella and Parmesan and sprinkle over. Bake for 15–20 minutes until crisp and golden. Serve immediately.

Red Onion, Gorgonzola and Sage

This topping combines the richness of Gorgonzola with the earthy flavours of sage and sweet red onions.

Serves 4

INGREDIENTS
1 quantity Basic or Superquick Pizza
  Dough
30 ml/2 tbsp Garlic Oil
2 small red onions
150 g/5 oz Gorgonzola *piccante*
2 garlic cloves
10 ml/2 tsp chopped fresh sage
black pepper

sage

Gorgonzola

red onions

garlic

Garlic Oil

1 Preheat the oven to 220°C/425°F/ Gas 7. Divide the dough into eight pieces and roll out each one on a lightly floured surface to a small oval about 5 mm/¼ in thick. Place well apart on two greased baking sheets and prick with a fork. Brush the bases well with 15 ml/1 tbsp of the Garlic Oil.

2 Halve, then slice the onions into thin wedges. Scatter over the pizza bases.

3 Remove the rind from the Gorgonzola. Cut the cheese into small cubes, then scatter it over the onions.

4 Cut the garlic lengthways into thin strips and sprinkle over, along with the sage. Drizzle the remaining oil on top and grind over plenty of black pepper. Bake for 10–15 minutes until crisp and golden. Serve immediately.

73

Onion and Three Cheese

You can use any combination of cheese you like. Edam and Cheddar both have good flavours and melting properties.

Serves 3–4

INGREDIENTS
45 ml/3 tbsp olive oil
3 medium onions, sliced
1 pizza base, 25–30 cm/10–12 in
   diameter
4 small tomatoes, peeled, seeded and
   cut into thin wedges
30 ml/2 tbsp chopped fresh basil
115 g/4 oz Dolcelatte
150 g/5 oz mozzarella
115 g/4 oz Red Leicester
black pepper
fresh basil leaves, to garnish

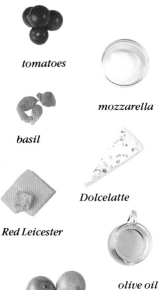

tomatoes

mozzarella

basil

Dolcelatte

Red Leicester

olive oil

onions

1 Preheat the oven to 220°C/425°F/ Gas 7. Heat 30 ml/2 tbsp of the oil in a frying pan, add the onions and gently fry for about 10 minutes, stirring occasionally. Leave to cool.

2 Brush the pizza base with the remaining oil. Spoon over the onions and tomatoes, then scatter over the basil.

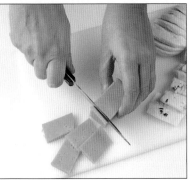

3 Thinly slice the cheeses and arrange over the tomatoes and onions.

4 Grind over plenty of black pepper and bake for 15–20 minutes until crisp and golden. Garnish with basil leaves and serve immediately.

Feta, Roasted Garlic and Oregano

This is a pizza for garlic lovers! Mash down the cloves as you eat – they should be soft and will have lost their pungency.

Serves 4

INGREDIENTS

1 medium garlic bulb, unpeeled
45 ml/3 tbsp olive oil
1 medium red pepper, quartered and seeded
1 medium yellow pepper, quartered and seeded
2 plum tomatoes
1 quantity Basic or Superquick Pizza Dough
175 g/6 oz feta, crumbled
black pepper
15–30 ml/1–2 tbsp chopped fresh oregano, to garnish

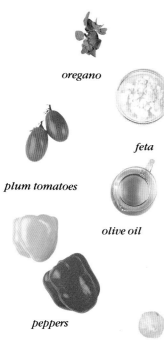

oregano

feta

plum tomatoes

olive oil

peppers

garlic bulb

1 Preheat the oven to 220°C/425°F/ Gas 7. Break the garlic into cloves, discarding the outer papery layers. Toss in 15 ml/1 tbsp of the oil.

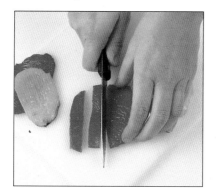

2 Place the peppers skin-side up on a baking sheet and grill until the skins are evenly charred. Place in a covered bowl for 10 minutes, then peel off the skins. Cut the flesh into strips.

3 Put the tomatoes in a bowl and pour over boiling water. Leave for 30 seconds, then plunge into cold water. Peel, seed and roughly chop the flesh. Divide the dough into four pieces and roll out each one on a lightly floured surface to a 13 cm/5 in circle.

4 Place the dough circles well apart on two greased baking sheets, then push up the dough edges to form a thin rim. Brush with half the remaining oil and scatter over the chopped tomatoes. Top with the peppers, crumbled feta and garlic cloves. Drizzle over the remaining oil and season with black pepper. Bake for 15–20 minutes until crisp and golden. Garnish with chopped oregano and serve immediately.

Spring Vegetable and Pine Nuts

This colourful pizza is well worth the time it takes to prepare. You can vary the ingredients according to availability.

Serves 2–3

INGREDIENTS
1 pizza base, 25–30 cm/10–12 in
    diameter
45 ml/3 tbsp Garlic Oil
1 quantity Tomato Sauce
4 spring onions
2 courgettes
1 leek
115 g/4 oz asparagus tips
15 ml/1 tbsp chopped fresh oregano
30 ml/2 tbsp pine nuts
50 g/2 oz mozzarella, grated
30 ml/2 tbsp freshly grated Parmesan
black pepper

Parmesan

mozzarella

Tomato Sauce

spring onions

leek

courgette

asparagus   *pine nuts*

1 Preheat the oven to 220°C/425°F/ Gas 7. Brush the pizza base with 15 ml/1 tbsp of the Garlic Oil, then spread over the Tomato Sauce.

2 Slice the spring onions, courgettes, leek and asparagus.

3 Heat half the remaining Garlic Oil in a frying pan and stir-fry the vegetables for 3–5 minutes.

4 Arrange the vegetables over the Tomato Sauce.

5 Sprinkle the oregano and pine nuts over the pizza.

6 Mix together the mozzarella and Parmesan and sprinkle over. Drizzle over the remaining Garlic Oil and season with black pepper. Bake for 15–20 minutes until crisp and golden. Serve immediately.

Spinach and Ricotta Panzerotti

These make great party food to serve with drinks or as tasty appetizers for a crowd.

Makes 20–24

INGREDIENTS

115 g/4 oz frozen chopped spinach, defrosted and squeezed dry
50 g/2 oz ricotta
50 g/2 oz freshly grated Parmesan
generous pinch freshly grated nutmeg
2 quantities Basic or Superquick Pizza Dough
1 egg white, lightly beaten
vegetable oil for deep-frying
salt and black pepper

nutmeg

ricotta

vegetable oil

egg

frozen spinach

Parmesan

1 Place the spinach, ricotta, Parmesan, nutmeg and seasoning in a bowl and beat until smooth.

2 Roll out the dough on a lightly floured surface to about 3 mm/⅛ in thick. Using a 7.5 cm/3 in plain round cutter stamp out 20–24 circles.

3 Spread a teaspoon of spinach mixture over one half of each circle.

4 Brush the edges of the dough with a little egg white.

5 Fold the dough over the filling and press the edges firmly together to seal.

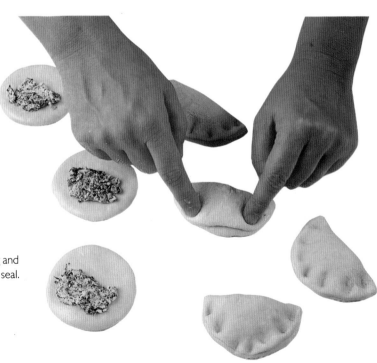

COOK'S TIP
Do serve these as soon as possible after frying, they will become much less appetizing if left to cool.

6 Heat the oil in a large heavy-based pan or deep-fat fryer to 180°C/350°F. Deep-fry the panzerotti a few at a time for 2–3 minutes until golden. Drain on kitchen paper and serve immediately.

Smoked Salmon Pizzettes

Mini pizzas topped with smoked salmon, crème fraîche and lumpfish roe make an extra special party canapé.

Makes 10–12

INGREDIENTS

1 quantity Basic or Superquick Pizza
  Dough
15 ml/1 tbsp snipped fresh chives
15 ml/1 tbsp olive oil
75–115 g/3–4 oz smoked salmon, cut
  into strips
60 ml/4 tbsp crème fraîche
30 ml/2 tbsp black lumpfish roe
chives, to garnish

crème fraîche

olive oil

smoked salmon

chives

black lumpfish roe

1 Preheat the oven to 200°C/400°F/ Gas 6. Knead the dough gently, adding the chives until evenly mixed.

2 Roll out the dough on a lightly floured surface to about 3 mm/⅛ in thick. Using a 7.5 cm/3 in plain round cutter stamp out 10–12 circles.

3 Place the bases well apart on two greased baking sheets, prick all over with a fork, then brush with the oil. Bake for 10–15 minutes until crisp and golden.

4 Arrange the smoked salmon on top, then spoon on the crème fraîche. Spoon a tiny amount of lumpfish roe in the centre and garnish with chives. Serve immediately.

Sun-dried Tomatoes, Basil and Olive Pizza Bites

This quick and easy recipe uses scone pizza dough with the addition of chopped fresh basil.

Makes 24

INGREDIENTS

18–20 fresh basil leaves
1 quantity Scone Pizza Dough
30 ml/2 tbsp tomato oil (from jar of
  sun-dried tomatoes)
1 quantity Tomato Sauce
115 g/4 oz (drained weight) sun-dried
  tomatoes in oil, chopped
10 pitted black olives, chopped
50 g/2 oz mozzarella, grated
30 ml/2 tbsp freshly grated Parmesan
shredded basil leaves, to garnish

1 Preheat the oven to 220°C/425°F/ Gas 7. Tear the basil leaves into small pieces. Add half to the scone mix before mixing to a soft dough. Set aside the remainder.

mozzarella

black olives

Parmesan

Tomato Sauce

tomato oil

basil

sun-dried tomatoes

2 Knead the dough gently on a lightly floured surface until smooth. Roll out and use to line a 30 × 18 cm/12 × 7 in Swiss-roll tin. Push up the edges to make a thin rim.

3 Brush the base with 15 ml/1 tbsp of the tomato oil, then spread over the Tomato Sauce. Scatter over the sun-dried tomatoes, olives and remaining basil.

4 Mix together the mozzarella and Parmesan and sprinkle over. Drizzle over the remaining tomato oil. Bake for about 20 minutes. Cut lengthways and across into 24 bite-size pieces. Garnish with extra shredded basil leaves and serve immediately.

Farmhouse Pizza

This is the ultimate party pizza. Served cut into fingers, it is ideal for a crowd.

Serves 8

INGREDIENTS

90 ml/6 tbsp olive oil
225 g/8 oz button mushrooms, sliced
2 quantities Basic or Superquick Pizza
   Dough
1 quantity Tomato Sauce
300 g/10 oz mozzarella, thinly sliced
115 g/4 oz wafer-thin smoked ham
   slices
6 bottled artichoke hearts in oil,
   drained and sliced
50 g/2 oz can anchovy fillets, drained
   and halved lengthways
10 pitted black olives, halved
30 ml/2 tbsp chopped fresh oregano
45 ml/3 tbsp freshly grated Parmesan
black pepper

1 Preheat the oven to 220°C/425°F/ Gas 7. Heat 30 ml/2 tbsp of the oil in a large frying pan, add the mushrooms and fry for about 5 minutes until all the juices have evaporated. Leave to cool.

2 Roll out the dough on a lightly floured surface to a 30 × 25 cm/12 × 10 in rectangle. Transfer to a greased baking sheet, then push up the dough edges to make a thin rim. Brush with 30 ml/2 tbsp of the oil.

3 Spread over the Tomato Sauce.

mozzarella

anchovy fillets

artichoke hearts

smoked ham

olive oil

Tomato Sauce

black olives

button mushrooms

4 Arrange the sliced mozzarella over the sauce.

5 Scrunch up the ham and arrange on top with the artichoke hearts, mushrooms and anchovies.

6 Dot with the olives, then sprinkle over the oregano and Parmesan. Drizzle over the remaining oil and season with black pepper. Bake for about 25 minutes until crisp and golden. Serve immediately.

Feta, Pimiento and Pine Nut

Delight your guests with these tempting pizzas.
Substitute goat's cheese for the feta if you prefer.

Makes 24

INGREDIENTS
2 quantities Basic or Superquick Pizza
    Dough
60 ml/4 tbsp olive oil
30 ml/2 tbsp black olive tapenade
175 g/6 oz feta
1 large canned pimiento, drained
30 ml/2 tbsp chopped fresh thyme
30 ml/2 tbsp pine nuts
black pepper
thyme sprigs, to garnish

pimiento

thyme

feta cheese

tapenade

pine nuts

1 Preheat the oven to 220°C/425°F/
Gas 7. Divide the dough into 24 pieces
and roll out each one on a lightly floured
surface to a small oval, about 3 mm/⅛ in
thick. Place well apart on greased baking
sheets and prick all over with a fork.
Brush with 30 ml/2 tbsp of the oil.

2 Spread a thin layer of the black olive
tapenade on each oval and crumble over
the feta.

3 Cut the pimiento into thin strips and
pile on top.

4 Sprinkle each one with thyme and
pine nuts. Drizzle over the remaining oil
and grind over plenty of black pepper.
Bake for 10–15 minutes until crisp and
golden. Garnish with thyme sprigs and
serve immediately.

Mozzarella, Anchovy and Pesto

These unusual pizzas combine the piquancy of olives and capers with anchovies and mozzarella.

Makes 24

INGREDIENTS
2 ready-to-cook pizza bases, about
    20 cm/8 in diameter
60 ml/4 tbsp olive oil
30 ml/2 tbsp red pesto
12 pitted black olives
75 g/3 oz mozzarella, cubed
50 g/2 oz (drained weight) sun-dried
    tomatoes in oil, chopped
30–45/2–3 tbsp capers
50 g/2 oz can anchovy fillets, drained
    and roughly chopped
30 ml/2 tbsp freshly grated Parmesan
parsley sprigs, to garnish

parsley

sun-dried tomatoes

mozzarella

capers

olive oil

black olives

red pesto

anchovy fillets

1 Preheat the oven to 220°C/425°F/
Gas 7. Using a 5 cm/2 in plain round
cutter stamp out 24 rounds from the
pizza bases. Place the rounds on two
greased baking sheets.

2 Brush the bases with 30 ml/2 tbsp of
the oil, then spread over the pesto.

3 Cut the olives into quarters
lengthways, then scatter over the bases
with the mozzarella, sun-dried tomatoes,
capers and anchovies.

4 Sprinkle over the Parmesan and
drizzle over the remaining oil. Bake for
8–10 minutes until crisp and golden.
Garnish with parsley sprigs and serve
immediately.

Sun-dried Tomato Bread

This savoury bread tastes delicious on its own, but it also makes exceptional sandwiches.

Makes 1 loaf

INGREDIENTS
375 g/13 oz/3¼ cups strong white
    flour
5 ml/1 tsp salt
10 ml/2 tsp easy-blend dried yeast
50 g/2 oz (drained weight) sun-dried
    tomatoes in oil, chopped
175 ml/6 fl oz/¾ cup lukewarm water
75 ml/5 tbsp lukewarm olive oil, plus
    extra for brushing
plain flour for dusting

water

strong white flour

olive oil

easy-blend yeast

sun-dried tomatoes

salt

1 Sift the flour and salt into a large mixing bowl.

2 Stir in the yeast and sun-dried tomatoes.

3 Make a well in the centre of the dry ingredients. Pour in the water and oil, and mix until the ingredients come together and form a soft dough.

4 Turn the dough on to a lightly floured surface and knead for about 10 minutes.

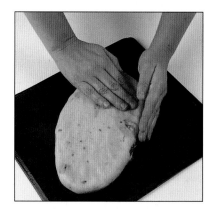

5 Shape into an oblong loaf, without making the top too smooth, and place on a greased baking sheet. Brush the top with oil, cover with clear film, then leave to rise in a warm place for about 1 hour.

6 Meanwhile, preheat the oven to 220°C/425°F/Gas 7. Remove the clear film, then sprinkle the top of the loaf lightly with flour. Bake for 30–40 minutes until the loaf sounds hollow when tapped on the bottom. Serve warm.

Rosemary and Sea Salt Focaccia

Focaccia is an Italian flat bread made with olive oil. Here it is given added flavour with rosemary and coarse sea salt.

Makes 1 loaf

INGREDIENTS
350 g/12 oz/3 cups plain flour
2.5 ml/½ tsp salt
10 ml/2 tsp easy-blend dried yeast
about 250 ml/8 fl oz/1 cup lukewarm
    water
45 ml/3 tbsp olive oil
1 small red onion
leaves from 1 large rosemary sprig
5 ml/1 tsp coarse sea salt

coarse sea salt

water

olive oil

plain flour

easy-blend yeast

red onion

rosemary

1 Sift the flour and salt into a large mixing bowl. Stir in the yeast, then make a well in the centre of the dry ingredients. Pour in the water and 30 ml/2 tbsp of the oil. Mix well, adding a little more water if the mixture seems dry.

2 Turn the dough on to a lightly floured surface and knead for about 10 minutes until smooth and elastic.

3 Place the dough in a greased bowl, cover and leave in a warm place for about 1 hour until doubled in size. Knock back and knead the dough for 2–3 minutes.

4 Meanwhile, preheat the oven to 220°C/425°F/Gas 7. Roll out the dough to a large circle, about 1 cm/½ in thick, and transfer to a greased baking sheet. Brush with the remaining oil.

5 Halve the onion and slice into thin wedges. Sprinkle over the dough, with the rosemary and sea salt, pressing in lightly.

6 Using a finger make deep indentations in the dough. Cover the surface with greased clear film, then leave to rise in a warm place for 30 minutes. Remove the clear film and bake for 25–30 minutes until golden. Serve warm.

Mini Focaccia with Pine Nuts

Pine nuts add little bites of nutty texture to these mini focaccias.

Makes 4 mini loaves

INGREDIENTS
350 g/12 oz/3 cups plain flour
2.5 ml/½ tsp salt
10 ml/2 tsp easy-blend dried yeast
about 250 ml/8 fl oz/1 cup lukewarm
    water
45 ml/3 tbsp olive oil
45–60/3–4 tbsp pine nuts
10 ml/2 tsp coarse sea salt

water

sea salt

olive oil

plain flour

easy-blend yeast

pine nuts

1 Sift the flour and salt into a large mixing bowl. Stir in the yeast, then make a well in the centre of the dry ingredients. Pour in the water and 30 ml/2 tbsp of the oil. Mix well, adding more water if the mixture seems dry. Turn on to a lightly floured surface and knead for about 10 minutes until smooth and elastic. Place the dough in a greased bowl, cover and leave in a warm place for about 1 hour until doubled in size. Knock back and knead the dough for 2–3 minutes.

2 Divide the dough into four pieces.

3 Using your hands pat out each piece on greased baking sheets to a 10 × 7.5 cm/4 × 3 in oblong, rounded at the ends.

4 Scatter over the pine nuts and gently press them into the surface. Sprinkle with salt and brush with the remaining oil. Cover with greased clear film and leave to rise for about 30 minutes. Meanwhile, preheat the oven to 220°C/425°F/Gas 7. Remove the clear film and bake the focaccias for 15–20 minutes until golden. Serve warm.

Walnut Bread

The nutty flavour of this wonderfully textured bread is excellent. Try it toasted and topped with melting goat's cheese for a mouth-watering snack.

Makes 2 loaves

INGREDIENTS

600 g/1 lb 5 oz/4 cups strong white flour
10 ml/2 tsp salt
10 ml/2 tsp easy-blend dried yeast
150 g/5 oz/1¼ cups chopped walnuts
60 ml/4 tbsp chopped fresh parsley
400 ml/14 fl oz/1⅔ cups lukewarm water
60 ml/4 tbsp olive oil

strong white flour

olive oil

easy-blend yeast

parsley

walnuts

salt

1 Sift the flour and salt into a large mixing bowl. Stir in the yeast, walnuts and parsley.

2 Make a well in the centre of the dry ingredients. Pour in the water and oil and mix to a soft dough. Turn the dough on to a lightly floured surface and knead for about 10 minutes until smooth and elastic. Place in a greased bowl, cover and leave in a warm place for about 1 hour until doubled in size.

3 Knock back and knead the dough for 2–3 minutes. Divide in half and shape each piece into a thick roll about 18–20 cm/7–8 in long. Place on greased baking sheets, cover with clear film and leave to rise for about 30 minutes.

4 Meanwhile, preheat the oven to 220°C/425°F/Gas 7. Remove the clear film, then lightly slash the top of each loaf. Bake for 10 minutes, then reduce the oven temperature to 180°C/350°F/Gas 4 and bake for a further 25–30 minutes until the loaves sound hollow when tapped. Serve warm.

Olive Bread

Green olives are added to heighten the flavour of this moist bread. Use a combination of green and black olives if you prefer.

Makes 2 loaves

INGREDIENTS
700 g/1½ lb/6 cups strong white flour
5 ml/1 tsp salt
sachet of easy-blend dried yeast
15 ml/1 tbsp chopped fresh oregano
350 ml/12 fl oz/1½ cups lukewarm
   water
105 ml/7 tbsp olive oil
about 30 pitted green olives

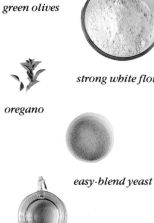

green olives

strong white flour

oregano

easy-blend yeast

olive oil

salt

1 Sift the flour and salt into a large mixing bowl. Stir in the yeast and oregano.

2 Measure the water into a jug, then stir in 90 ml/6 tbsp of the oil. Make a well in the centre of the dry ingredients, pour in the liquid and mix to a soft dough.

3 Turn the dough on to a lightly floured surface and knead for about 10 minutes until smooth and elastic. Place in a greased bowl, cover with clear film and leave in a warm place for about 1 hour until doubled in size.

4 Knock back and knead the dough for 2–3 minutes. Divide in half, then press the dough on greased baking sheets into two ovals, about 1 cm/½ in thick.

5 Using a clean finger make about 15 deep indentations over the surface of each loaf. Press an olive into each indentation.

6 Brush the loaves with the remaining oil, cover with clear film and leave to rise for 30 minutes. Meanwhile, preheat the oven to 220°C/425°F/Gas 7. Remove the clear film and bake for 20–25 minutes until the loaves sound hollow when tapped. Serve warm.

Saffron and Basil Breadsticks

Saffron lends its delicate aroma and flavour, as well as rich yellow colour, to these tasty breadsticks.

Makes 32

INGREDIENTS
generous pinch saffron strands
450 g/1 lb/4 cups strong white flour
5 ml/1 tsp salt
10 ml/2 tsp easy-blend dried yeast
300 ml/½ pint/1¼ cups lukewarm
    water
45 ml/3 tbsp olive oil
45 ml/3 tbsp chopped fresh basil

strong white flour

water

olive oil

easy-blend yeast

basil

saffron strands

salt

1 Infuse the saffron strands in 30 ml/2 tbsp hot water for 10 minutes.

2 Sift the flour and salt into a large mixing bowl. Stir in the yeast, then make a well in the centre of the dry ingredients. Pour in the water and saffron liquid and start to mix a little.

3 Add the oil and basil and continue to mix to a soft dough.

4 Turn out and knead the dough on a lightly floured surface for about 10 minutes until smooth and elastic. Place in a greased bowl, cover with clear film and leave for about 1 hour until it has doubled in size.

5 Knock back and knead the dough on a lightly floured surface for 2–3 minutes.

6 Preheat the oven to 220°C/425°F/ Gas 7. Divide the dough into 32 pieces and shape into long sticks. Place well apart on greased baking sheets, then leave for a further 15–30 minutes until they become puffy. Bake for about 15 minutes until crisp and golden. Serve warm.